WHAT I *love* ABOUT

GRAND PA

Fill in the love
AND GIVE TO GRANDPA

ISBN-13: 978-1-56383-629-9
Item #4102

**Printed in the USA
by G&R Publishing Co.**

Distributed By:

507 Industrial Street
Waverly, IA 50677

www.cqbookstore.com

gifts@cqbookstore.com

CQ Products

CQ Products

@cqproducts

@cqproducts

This book is for

Theo

From

?

6 years old

♡ ABOUT MY GRANDPA ♡

Your name is ~~Theodore Jon~~.

I think you are 66 years old.

You are as tall as a half of

A bus and your hair is

gray.

your smile looks like __mine.__

_____

and your eyes are __brownish__

__gree__ .

♡ **YOU ARE MY GRANDPA!** ♡

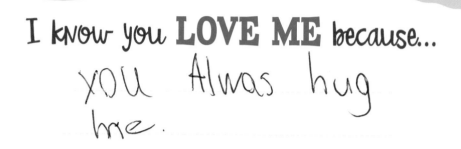

I know you **LOVE ME** because...
YOU Almas hug
me.

I'm happiest
when we...
Play
CACh
With
the
footBall

THINGS ABOUT ME

My favorite color is... Red

I like this zoo animal best...
A Tiger

If I could have any pet in the world, I would choose a...
A ciddy.

When I grow up, I hope to be...
A pokemon traner.

Here's something I would like to know about you...

How you play football so good.

You like to
tease me about...

I like to
tease you about...

pop

Grandpa, wanna hear a joke?

GENTLE
GRACIOUS
BRAVE
FUNNY
DEDICATED
HAPPY
ADORED

You're all these and so much more!

I love it when you
visit because...

My FAVORITE place
in your house is...
the yard.

My favorite thing to
help you with is...
?

Something **FUNNY** that happened
when we were together...

when you call
me boopedrose

You always laugh
whenever I...

I giggle when I
think about your...

I LOVE
YOU BECAUSE...

You think I'm...

You let me...

You take the time to...

You're patient when I...

You understand when...

You help me...

...YOU'RE YOU!

WORLD'S BEST GRANDPA

You're the best at...

Here are some questions
I'd like to ask you...

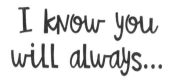
I know you
will always...

I know you will never...

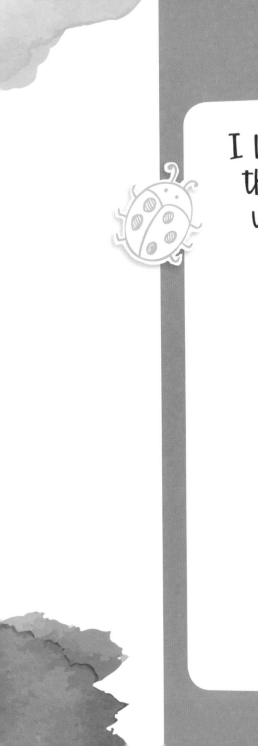

I like sharing
these things
with you...

I think you're
smart because you know...

I'd like it if you taught
me how to...

Maybe someday I could
teach you how to...

IF GRANDPA can't fix it, NO ONE CAN

I think you're amazing because you can fix...

Remember when we...

Sometime I'd like to
do this with you...

The **BEST** toys at your house are...

the blue football.

When you were my age, I think your favorite toys might have been...

Grandpa, here's what my
favorite toys look like...

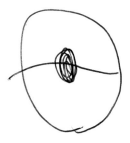

Your hugs are like...

They make me feel...

If I had to guess, I'd say you've hugged me _____ times.

Whenever you see
me, you...

Whenever I see you, I...

Here's a story about you...
~~after the~~ one time at nesgain We Were ther and We did not have A ball then WeSAW A Store We baut A blue football. We play'd cach We had fun!!!!!!!

The End

GRANDPAS
are a
DELIGHTFUL
BLEND *of*
HELPING HANDS,
GOOD STORIES,
LAUGHTER, *and lots*
OF LOVE

Grandpa, if you had a
SUPERPOWER, it would be...

What I like most about my

birthday is _____

and _____.

My favorite kind of cake is _____

_____ with _____

frosting. I can hardly wait until

my next birthday!

This is what I think you wish for when you blow out your birthday candles...

The best gift you ever gave me was...

DID YOU KNOW...

My favorite holiday with you is

_____

because we _____

_____ .

The house always smells like

_____ .

We eat _____

_____ .

You make this day special by

_____ .

IF YOU DON'T BELIEVE IN HEROES, YOU HAVEN'T MET MY GRANDPA

Grandpa, I think you're SUPER because...

Grandpa, here's how my smile looks when we're together...

Something about me
that looks like you...

You ALWAYS say
this to me...

I love playing this
with you...

because...

I always win
when we play...

You always win
when we play...

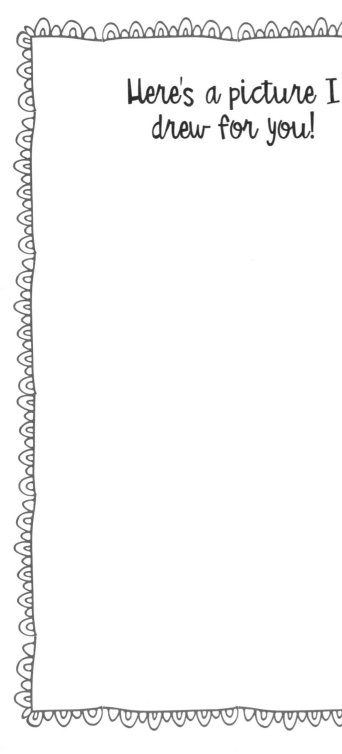

Here's a picture I
drew for you!

I do not like these things...

But I really love...

you do not like these things...

But you really love...

4 things
that make my heart happy...

1.

2.

3.

4.

I ♡ LOVE

THAT YOU'RE MY

Grandpa

Your
makes me smile because...

I think your favorite
hobby is...

I like to watch you...

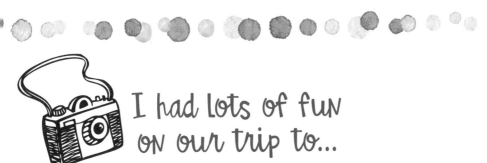

I had lots of fun
on our trip to...

Grandpas
are there to help
children
get into the mischief
they haven't
thought
of YET!

I LOVE to do these things when we're together...

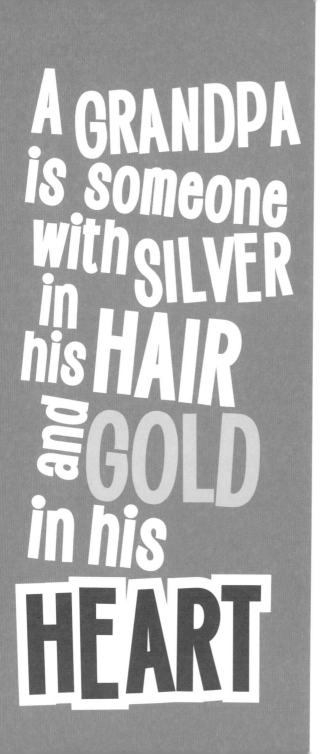

A GRANDPA is someone with SILVER in his HAIR and GOLD in his HEART

I know you're young
at heart because...

I like it when you
tell me stories about...

I love it when you read
me these books...

I had fun when you
taught me how to...

GRANDPA

Dear _____,

(my name for you)

I love you! You're better than

mud puddles, ice cream, and _____

_____.

You're silliest when you _____

_____.

When you laugh, I laugh because

--•

I would ----------------------------------

all day long just to make you

smile. I hope I see you soon!

Love ----------------------------------

I'm your little

--•

A child needs a grandpa
to teach them what they know.
To always be a part of them,
no matter where they go.
So Grandpa, here's my little hand,
I'll put it on your heart.
So even if we're far away,
we'll never be apart.

your handprint here

Here's a picture of
Grandpa and me...